THE PT BUSINESS MAP

BEGINNING YOUR JOURNEY TO BECOMING
AN EMPOWERED OWNER

DR. AMY KONVALIN, MPT, DMT,
PHD, OCS, FAAOMPT

KNOTTED ROAD PRESS, INC.

The PT Business Map
Beginning Your Journey to Becoming an Empowered Owner

Copyright © 2019 Amy Konvalin
All rights reserved
Published by Knotted Road Press
www.KnottedRoadPress.com

ISBN: 978-1-68641-227-1

Cover art:
ID 143347561 © Parviz Narimanov - Dreamstime.com
African photo - Sara Kirkland

Head shot: Ashley Creek

Cover and interior design copyright © 2019 Knotted Road Press
http://www.KnottedRoadPress.com

All rights reserved. Except for brief quotations in critical articles or reviews, the purchaser or reader may not modify, copy, distribute, transmit, display perform, reproduce, publish, license, create derivative works from, transfer or sell any information contained in this book without the express written permission of Amy Konvalin or Knotted Road Press. Requests to use or quote this material for any purpose should be addressed to Amy Konvalin.

INTRODUCTION

"We need to discuss my exit strategy"

As those words fell out of my mouth, my mouth fell to the floor. I had just quit my job with NO PLAN, NO safety net, and NOWHERE TO GO! What was I going to tell my husband?

But what brought me to that drastic point? Before I started at my previous office, I interviewed with Newt (name changed to protect the innocent. If you want the entire story then buy me a beer and we can talk) for six hours total. I wanted to ensure that he was clear on who I was and how I practiced. I wanted to come in and create a positive impact in the clinic he had run for twenty two years at that point.

However, I needed to do it my way. I needed one-on-one appointments for one hour with each patient. I did not have to pass them off to techs or aides to complete their exercises or treatment. I could see them through from beginning to end. No pressure to use ultrasound and E-stim. They were both present in the clinic so the option was always available.

I did my own billing and justified the codes I used. This can be tricky because different people have a different

Introduction

understanding of codes and billing. But I was paid on a percentage basis at this company, so I was free to bill the best way I knew. I could maintain my personal ethics and I was not pushed to do something I felt wasn't right.

All that changed that one fate-filled day in April. Everything had been humming along as far as I could tell. We had started with a new documentation system about a year before, which was a challenge. Newt had hired a new Physical Therapist so now there were three of us. That was a really big deal for him because it was the first time he had three Physical Therapists working in the clinic.

I will never know what caused him to change his mind about our agreement. I was bringing in more money than anyone else in the clinic. My clients were extremely happy and doing really well. But, that day in April, Newt had called me into his office to say that everything needed to change.

More patients.

More use of aides/techs.

More ultrasound/E-stim.

Less hands on with patients.

As soon as he finished his statement, I uttered those destiny filled words. "We need to discuss my exit strategy". Newt asked me if I was quitting and what I was going to do. I told him right there on the spot without any preparation or research that I was going to open my own clinic.

Truly I had no other place to go. I wanted to work close to home and stop the insane commuting I had done previous to that. I knew the other clinics in town were not going to provide me with the amazing deal I had at my old clinic. None of them would allow me one hour treatments with each patient. I knew. I had already interviewed with them prior to starting there.

So, the only thing left for me to do was go out and try it on my own. But, how do you take the first step? What is

Introduction

even required to open a Physical Therapy clinic? And, what if you don't want to open a clinic but instead want to do a concierge practice? What options are out there?

I searched the internet to find some resources. Someone to tell me what the next step was. I couldn't find anything! No books, no websites, no resources to tell me what I should be doing. It was frustrating and I was lost. Completely on my own navigating this entirely new world.

I am now two years into my new business. Boy, have I learned a lot! There have been really good times and there have been really low times. There are patients who remind me why I did this in the first and patients who are frustrated by my current system.

In calendar year #2, I hit my goal of making as much as I was making at my previous jobs. In my second year! That has earned me the right to shoot for a 3rd year which I am hoping will be even better.

Before I embark on that 3rd year, I wanted to write down how it all started. I wanted to document those first few steps for you. I wanted to write the book that I wish I had had on that fate-filled day. The book that will help YOU to create success on your own terms.

This book is filled with the first steps to opening a business. The legal aspects. The financial aspects. The logistical aspects. It is filled with questions you should ask yourself (and answer!) before you open your doors. It lays out my template for success. I realize that the way I did it may not work for you. That's okay. In this book I will further lay out my decision making process. You can make the decisions that work best for your company.

This book is an outline for you to follow to successfully open the doors to your very own Physical Therapy practice. To find the freedom to work the way you feel is best for the

Introduction

population you serve. I know you can do it! If you have the desire in your heart then the rest is just logistics.

How To Use This Book

First, take a deep breath. You are embarking on a marathon. Starting your own company is not a sprint that you are going to finish any time soon. Once you make it through the first step the next one is waiting for you. So remember to breathe and enjoy the journey. You will accomplish great things one step at a time.

Second, don't stay in one place too long. As we travel through this book together, you will find there are many decision steps and many action steps. There are things you need to make decisions on before you can perform the required action. Take the time to decide on an appropriate course of action but don't stay in one place for too long. Which leads to #3.

The third and perhaps most important point is - avoid analysis paralysis. You can spend weeks or months thinking up just the right name for your clinic or designing the best logo the world has ever seen. Perhaps you have that kind of time. You may be reading this book several years before you want to open your own place. Or you may be looking to open your doors as soon as possible and these steps are slowing you down. Remember, for many of these things perfection is not required. Make a decision. Stand by it. Learn from it in the future. Just don't stay here! Move forward.

If you find yourself stuck in one chapter or on one question, feel free to move on. Give yourself some space from the question and the answer that is eluding you. You may find the answer in the next chapter. Or you may find yourself changing your mind. All of this is normal!

Just keep moving forward. You have totally got this!

You will find some chapters and discussions are small.

Introduction

For instance, deciding if your company should be a PLLC or an S-corp. I spent HOURS agonizing over this decision and researching it but have come to realize that it's actually a pretty simple decision. However I did not spend much time working on my marketing before I opened my doors. Hence the incredibly long marketing section! I have learned from my mistakes and now realize that I should have spent way more time thinking about the marketing aspect BEFORE I opened my doors.

Again, this is the book that I wish I had when I quit my job suddenly. It was written to tell you all the things that I wish I had known. And to help you find your own answers to the questions that are presented throughout. I only put what I feel are the essential first steps in this book. The information you need to make the decisions you need to make in order to start your company.

Editorial note from my husband: My better half read a draft of this book and really wanted me to point something out to you. Before you start on this journey, make sure all the people who you are financially responsible to/for/with are on board with the plan. Most likely you will have a few years of making less than you previously did while you build the company you want to build. That can be tough on relationships. If your financial partners are not in agreement with your decision to open a company then more discussion needs to happen around that. Because there will be days (maybe weeks!) where you will feel like giving up. You need to have someone there to lift you up, remind you why you started this journey, and believe in your dream.

All right, is everyone on board? Let's get to this!

A Word of Advice From My Hair Dresser

Do you absolutely love your hair dresser? I love mine! Kelsey and I have been together for twelve years and counting. We have been through everything together and she

Introduction

is one of my biggest cheerleaders. No wonder I travel thirty minutes each way to see her.

Kelsey opened up her own shop six years into our relationship. After she had been open for a couple of years we were talking about business ownership. I did not yet have my own place but Kelsey knew it was going to be in my future. One day, she spun around my chair, looked me deep in the eyes and said:

"Whatever you do when you open your business, Amy, do NOT have a partner. Do it on your own".

Again, at this point I wasn't even thinking about opening my own company but her intensity made her words stick with me. When I abruptly quit my job I remembered what Kelsey had said. I did not even try to find a partner. Now I am glad that I have struggled through on my own.

Would a partner have pointed out some of my early mistakes? Potentially, yes. Would we have ended up fighting like cats and dogs? Probably, yes. I figure it's like living with your best friend. You shouldn't do that. I made that mistake in college and lost my best friend for several years. Luckily, we both grew up and reunited as adults.

Don't start your business with a partner.

Don't live with your best friend.

1

WHAT'S YOUR NAME?

Way to start out with an easy question, right? I know, but it will be critical for when you are moving forward with everything else. You will need to know your name to create legal documents, signage for the building, letterhead, business cards, the list goes on. Your name is important, so why not start with the important things first.

Your name is going to be with you through the course of your company. Of course, you can always change your name but that makes it harder for people to find you in the future. Once you get name recognition in your town, you don't want to lose it by changing your name. Only 80's rock stars get away with that!

So, choose your name very wisely. It will be with you for the long term and you want it to truly reflect who you are as a company.

Some people choose to use the name they were born with. That certainly makes it an easy choice and you can skip the rest of this chapter and move straight to Chapter 2. You do not get to collect $200 – sorry. Using your own name is extremely popular with Physical Therapy practices right now. You can use either your first name, your last name, or both.

In fact, the clinic I currently operate out of was formerly a Physical Therapy clinic that used the owner's first name. "Kevin's Manual Therapy" was a successful insurance-based practice. Kevin actually left my space to move into more of an "L&I" based clinic with a doctor. But people certainly knew his name! Having his name in the clinic title gave him personal name recognition and clinic name recognition. This can be a bonus as you are starting out in private practice.

I know many, many successful business that were built off of a person's name. They have successfully grown to have multiple employees where the owner is more running the company as opposed to seeing the patients. This is a simple way to come up with a name and chances are very good that the name is not already taken.

Another successful strategy for naming your company is the name of your town and "Physical Therapy". This has a proven track record of success time and time again. In fact, when I was deciding on my own name I spoke with the owner of Maple Valley Acupuncture. I asked her what she thought was the secret to her success and she said her name. You see, if anyone searches for "Your town" and "Physical Therapy" your name is going to come up first. It is automatic SEO love. If this option is not already taken, I highly encourage it.

What if you name your clinic after your town and decide you want to open a new clinic in a new town down the road? Again, you can use the name of the new town you are in and "Physical Therapy". You will get the SEO love for the new town, too. However, you will initially lose the name recognition from your first clinic. Do you really need to think that far ahead? You may or you may not. It depends on what you are trying to create (which we will discuss more in Chapter 2).

Do NOT go searching on-line for names for Physical Therapy clinics. This will only frustrate you as you see names that have already been chosen.

DO make sure you check on-line that your name is not already being used. The last thing you want is to get all your business cards and printed materials up and running only to have someone come after you for name defamation. You can search for trademarked names on the Trademark Electronic Search System (TESS). This system allows you to search the United States Patent and Trademark Office database of registered trademarks and prior pending applications.

But don't stop there. I initially did search through the TESS system and found no one in the Federal or State system that had my proposed name. However, I did a quick on-line search and found a clinic not far away that had the name I wanted. Luckily I found it before I had set up the company and printed all the things that need to be printed! Make sure you search for your name on-line AFTER you have come up with a proposed name.

To emphasize this point just a little bit more – there is a local restaurant in my town that is great. Casual feel, good food, family friendly, and great drink menu. It is packed all the time! Rumor has it they received a cease and desist letter from a restaurant in Florida who had the same name. Of course, they could purchase the rights to the name for a large sum of money. Instead, the restaurant decided to change their name. Which meant that they had to change their sign out front, their menus, and all their advertising. This is not cheap! But I am sure that it cost less than paying the restaurant in Florida what they were asking for.

Point being – search for your proposed name on-line before you solidify your decision.

Another thought process for how to choose your name is by considering who you want to connect with. This is actually the process that I went through. For my clinic, I chose "Physical Therapy for EveryBODY". My goal with this name was to bring attention to the fact that every BODY is different and requires a different treatment plan. I wanted to separate myself from the Physical Therapy mills that push each patient through with the same treatment plan. You know the ones I am talking about. Oh, you have low back pain? Here is our low back pain program. Many patients have been disappointed with this form of treatment in the past and I wanted to differentiate myself from the mill type system. However, the marketing folks don't really like my name. They remind me that I don't treat every body, I have a specific target population that I really want to treat. Which is true for all of us. I still like my name but I do wish I had thought of some of these things beforehand. So I present them here for you to think about.

I do encourage you to spend some time in deep reflection about using the term "Physical Therapy" in your name. I have found that the mill type system of Physical Therapy that is so often found in our communities has been a detriment to my business. "Oh, I tried Physical Therapy and it doesn't work". I have heard this phrase over and over again. I have also heard from most of my patients "Well, what you do isn't really Physical Therapy. At least not a type that I have ever seen before". So I encourage you to think outside the box to find another term you might be able to use. Some suggestions:

Manual Therapy
Pediatric Therapy
Sports Therapy

I encourage you to take your time in picking a name for your future company. Choose a name, research on-line to make sure it is not already being used, and then live with the name to see how it feels. Test it out on a few friends or family members and see what they think. Because you are about to send it all over your community and the world via your website. You want to make sure that it truly represents you, your business, and who you serve.

Pro Tip: Since you are a Physical Therapist I want to remind you that your creative space may not actually be sitting in front of a computer or sitting down with a pad of paper. So many times I have been paralyzed by having to SIT down to type or put my words down on paper. For me, and perhaps for you, my creative space comes when I am outside running. When I need to really think through things, you will find me out on the trails running long distances with my dog. Being on the trail means that I don't have to worry about traffic and I can listen to some music and just go! So, honor where that creative space is for you. Where do you do your best thinking? Find that space or location and go to town!

Once you have chosen your name you are ready to get to work on your logo. Perhaps you are creative and want to design the logo on your own. Great, go forward and enjoy the process. You want to make sure that you are able to offer the logo in all the formats that will be needed in future marketing.

For the rest of us who have no idea what that last sentence means let me introduce to you your new on-line friends. There are great websites out there where you can hire people to do specific projects for you. They are not super expensive and they will save you massive amounts of time.

To have my logo designed, I got on Thumbtack and put in a request for a logo design. Multiple people responded with their prices for services offered. I was able to peruse their on-line portfolios to choose one who had a style that was consistent with what I was looking for. I connected with her through Thumbtack and accepted her bid. She sent me a questionnaire to fill out describing my company. After I had completed the questionnaire, she sent me three designs to give her feedback on. I hit the jackpot because I liked all three designs. I took the logo from one design and asked her to combine it with the font from another design. When she put the two together I had the logo I wanted. The entire process took under a week.

Many people I have met since opening my practice prefer the use of Fiverr. Again, an on-line option where you can choose the person you want to work with and see a portfolio of their work on-line. I haven't used them yet but for many it is the go-to option for anything that needs to be designed.

I would highly encourage you to look locally to see if there is another small business you can support in your own community. I will point this out repeatedly through the course of this book. Whenever there is someone local, I always choose that option. Why? It allows you to connect with another small business in your community. You never know where that connection may lead you to in the future.

Plus, I strongly believe that building up your local small business community gives your business a little extra something. After all, you want your clients to spend their health care dollars with you. Why wouldn't you demonstrate how your business spends your dollars locally? Perhaps you could find something a little cheaper on-line but is that the personality of your clinic you want out in the world? When someone compliments your logo and you are able to brag about the local small business person who made it for you there is a win-win situation.

Yes, I realize that it is not always possible to get what you need locally. Sometimes you have to go on-line or purchase from a big box store. But we want our clients to avoid the big box Physical Therapy clinics and go for the small guy. We should lead the way as much as possible. Supporting local small businesses will do a great deal for your own business.

Congratulations! The first chapter is down. You are on your way to creating a successful business. You have chosen your name and you are working on getting your logo designed. Now, before we go any further, let's take a look into a crystal ball and see where your clinic is in five years.

2

WHAT DO YOU WANT TO BUILD?

THIS CHAPTER IS GOING to help you make some big decisions about where you want your company to start and where you see it progressing to in the future. It's important to keep your eye on where you want to be in the future as it will be the basis for many decisions. So, as you move through this chapter and the beginning of your clinic, make sure to ask yourself:

What does my company look like in five years?

First you want to decide who the patient is that you are going to focus on. Yes, you need to choose one particular person to focus on. I recommend that you name this person, that you think about him/her as a real person. In fact, you can base this on a real patient you have had. This person should be your ideal patient. The person you get out of bed and cannot wait to see in the clinic. The person who always enjoys seeing you and telling all their friends about you. This is the person you want to spend your lifetime serving. They are out there and you need to find them.

Some questions you should be able to answer about this patron:

1. What is his/her name?
2. How old is he/she?
3. Are they married? Children? Grandchildren?
4. What do they do for work?
5. What do they do in their free time?
6. Where do they shop?
7. Where do they spend time on-line? What social media do they consume?
8. What are their dreams for the future?
9. What are their fears regarding those dreams?
10. What do they always say about you?

Seriously, you should stop here and take a few moments to write down the answers to these questions. It is imperative that you dial down your message to one specific person to start with. Then you know how to make all the other decisions moving forward. You can just ask yourself "what would (insert name) think of this?"

Some Physical Therapists at this point will get really frustrated and explain that they can treat everybody who has pain or movement dysfunction. And I get that. I really do get that! But, until you focus specifically on who you want to see and who you work well with, you won't get any patients. In one on-line group I am a part of the saying is: "the riches are in the niches". It will be no different for you.

Focus on the person who brings you great joy to see on your schedule. The one who you have a laugh with or who brings you homemade jam. The person who lights up your day. You are happy to see them and they are happy to see you. They talk about you to all their friends because they think you are amazing. And you always have such fun when you see them.

This focus on your ideal patient will help you to remain people-focused instead of diagnosis-focused. When we start talking about what diagnosis we treat, we often lose the attention of the very people we want to serve. Because they are more than just their diagnosis. THEY know that and deep down WE know that. We need to keep that at the center of our minds because we are building this company for them. We are keeping our eyes focused on the people we want to serve in order to provide the ultimate experience for them.

At the same time we are creating a company that serves us and where we are in our lives. We get to determine what it is we are looking for in starting a business.

Are you building a company or creating a job?

When you look at what you are doing five years in the future, are you running a company or do you have a job? Do you have employees that work for you or are you still hustling to see all the patients yourself while keeping up on scheduling and notes? Are you still alone in what you are doing or have you built a team that supports your vision?

Truly, both options are good and can create success for you on your terms. But you need to be super clear about what you are looking to create or else you may become frustrated in the process. What is your definition of success? Because owning your own business is like chasing a moving target. You need to know when you have hit your own personal success goals.

These success goals will be different for each person just as the ideal client is different for each person. Of course we are all different people with different goals. But you need to define success on your terms so you know when you have achieved those goals.

When I was starting out my goal was to replace my income from my previous job. Basically, I was creating a job for myself. There was no one in town who was going to allow me to treat one-on-one for one hour with each patient so I needed to create that environment on my own. This plan affected the decisions I made.

After I had been open for a couple of months, a friend approached me and asked if she could rent some space to launch her business. I was happy to have a roommate who had more business experience than me so I eagerly said yes. I gave her my front office and moved my desk into one off the treatment rooms. It created a bit of a weird situation when new patients came in but overall things worked out just fine. Eventually, she moved out and I took back my front office. Since then my patients have told me that they prefer me being in the front office. They know if I am not with a patient they will see me right when they walk in. If they don't see me, they know I am with a patient.

I didn't realize the unintended consequences of having my friend rent my front office. My patients felt like they were unsure if I was in the clinic or if it was my roommate there. It created uncertainty for them which is never what we want.

I was creating a job for myself. I saw an opportunity to get some help with rent and I seized on it. I did not think about the fact that I could not hire a front office person until my roommate moved out. I did not think about the uncertainty that my patient felt when they couldn't see me upon walking in. I was making decisions based on the goals that I had created for myself.

My second calendar year in business I met my personal goal. I had replaced my salary at my previous job. I was able to contribute to my family and pay some of the bills. I had doubled my income from the first year to the second. Which felt pretty good! Of course like any hard charging Physical Therapists I realized that I could do more good. There were more of my ideal patients out there who needed help. Which has changed my focus from creating a job (which I have already done) to creating a company.

This changes my decision making process as well. I moved into that front office area and am currently preparing it for hiring a front office person. I have bought furniture to prepare for a second Physical Therapist to come join me. Eventually I will have two Physical Therapists working full time and I will see patients part time while focusing more energy on running the company.

As you can see, my goal has shifted since I opened my company. This is actually the reason why I am writing this book right now. I want to document those first few steps to help others. I want to explain what it takes just to get the doors open before I forget. My job is turning into a company and I want to document the journey this far to help you start your journey.

Do you want to run a company or are you really looking to create a job? There is no right or wrong answer but you need to be honest with yourself. This will help direct your path and keep you making the correct decisions for yourself and your ideal patient. At the end of the day, that is all that matters.

Now, one caveat to that statement is if you are looking to start your own company in order to make more money. Please proceed carefully if that is truly your goal. In fact, I would say stop now if your only goal is to make more money. Because the truth is that you will make less money for a while. Perhaps for a long while! I am blessed that my company has replaced my salary from my previous employer in only two years. Some people struggle for a much longer amount of time.

Even more than that, future clients know when you are only in it for the money. It is a deterrent to them not only in finding you but choosing to continue to work with you as well. Your future clients want to feel special and valued. We all want to feel important in our own world. This means that our clients need to know that we value them far beyond the financial value they bring to our lives. That we value the opportunity to work with them and we enjoy celebrating their success with them.

Now, I do understand that the Doctors of Physical Therapy are graduating further in debt than many of us who graduated years ago. I can completely understand that when your debt is so large you feel your compensation should measure up. And I am sorry that the inequity between your debt from school and your salary is so extreme. However that is the environment we practice in these days. I do not recommend going into business to try and cure this inequity.

I do encourage you to take some time to consider the biggest question that will come up when you open up your clinic:

Do you take my insurance?

Are you going to be an in-network provider or an out of network (OON) provider? This question will be critical to so many decisions you are making moving forward that it needs to be at the very beginning of any book on opening a Physical Therapy clinic. It is extremely important to find your footing in this one particular area because it affects so much of how you build your company.

If you have been in the Physical Therapy business for any amount of time you have seen drastic changes in reimbursement. I started school one month before Medicare enforced therapy caps for the first time in 1998. Before this point, Medicare would pay for any therapy that was performed. After October 1998, there was a limit for outpatient orthopedic Physical Therapy. Over time this trickled down to other insurance companies.

Physical Therapists no longer control if they will get reimbursed for their services. And insurance reimbursement is a constantly moving target. Every year (every month?) the rules change and you have to change what you are doing to get reimbursed.

For eight years before I went out on my own, I was in a profit sharing business model. This meant that I was given a percentage of what was collected each month by the company I worked for. This also meant that I was intimately familiar with what was happening with insurance reimbursements for the patients I was working with. I saw the rise and fall as each billing office learned how to communicate with each insurance company. Truly, it is a full time job and people who truly understand billing are priceless!

This declining reimbursement is what led my boss to tell me that I needed to treat more patients in less time with more use of techs/aides. Newt was looking at the economics and he needed to keep his business open and making money. With a one hour appointment time, I was maxing out what the insurance would reimburse for after 30-45 minutes (2-3 units). Which meant that we were not getting paid for the last 15-30 minutes (1-2 units). If I changed my treatment times to be shorter than I could see more patients per day thereby increasing our reimbursement. But that didn't work for me or for my ideal client.

You see, my ideal client has many questions and wants to understand what is going on with their body. They want to know what I have found that day and how their body has changed since the previous visit. My ideal client wants to feel seen and heard each moment they are in my clinic. They want to have constant access to me with questions or concerns.

To keep the level of service that my ideal client wants and deserves, I opted to be out of network with insurance. I wanted to serve my client and not the insurance company. I do provide a super bill so that my clients can get reimbursed from their insurance. I also provide a list of questions that I recommend each person ask their insurance company as well as notes to the insurance company upon request to aid in reimbursement.

Looking at my ideal client and what they wanted from their Physical Therapy experience told me that I could not provide that experience while being in network with insurance. You cannot offer Nordstrom service at Walmart prices. I do not appeal to the masses and that is okay. I know who I want to serve and those people are finding me. Because they are my ideal clients, my day is a joy.

However, this company consumes my life. When I am waiting for my daughters to get out of dance I am talking to other parents about their children's issues and what can be done to help them. When I am shopping at the grocery store I am running into current and former patients. While I am out running on the trail I am running into other therapists and patients.

Owning a company is not a nine to five job. It is not something you leave at the office and can pick back up the next day. It is completely consuming. In fact, I was taking a continuing education class recently and ran into a colleague I had worked with a few years back. He was excited to hear about my company and let me go on and on about the good, the bad, and the ugly. At the end of our discussion he said "I would never open my own company". Why not, I asked, surprised because he is a great therapist. "I don't want it to consume my life. I like my work-life balance right now".

Are you ready for this company to consume your life?

If not, you may want to think again about your timing on opening your company. Perhaps this idea needs to be shelved for a couple of years until you are ready to be all in on working for yourself. If you strongly feel that now is the time but you don't want it to be an all-consuming experience you will need to put strong safeguards in place to protect your time. Scheduling your day will become imperative so you can focus on what you goals are to accomplish. You will need to guard against creep into your lifestyle.

Recently I found out about Gary Sinek and his idea of "Start with why". Before you move on to the next chapter, I recommend you go watch the video: https://www.youtube.com/watch?v=u4ZoJKF_VuA . It will help you gain some solid footing before we move onto finding the right location for your business. Figuring out your why and who you serve helps to make all the decisions easier moving forward.

Gary Sinek explains that "people don't buy what you do, they buy why you do it". In the video, he uses Apple as an example. Apple is able to sell us computers, MP3 players, cell phones– anything they want to sell us. Because Apple has convinced us of their 'why'. Apple believes in challenging the status quo and thinking differently. That appeals to us on a deep level and makes us trust Apple. Therefore, we are comfortable buying what they are selling.

Remember, you get to take all the time you want before you move on in this book. You may need to spend a few weeks here working on your why and who you serve, and what you want your company to become. That is fine. This is not a sprint but a marathon. Take your time in the beginning to make sure you are creating what you want and what is best for your ideal customer. In the long run, time put in now will save you time and money later.

And take a deep breath before we move on and discuss the location of your business. You are doing a great job. Keep going at a steady pace.

3

LOCATION, LOCATION, LOCATION

When I suddenly quit my job with no notice, I had no plan for where I would open up a clinic. And no clue how to make that decision. So here are some questions to help you make the best decision for your business.

Question #1 – Clinic based, home based, or mobile company?

We are all familiar with the clinic based model where patients come to us. This includes renting a space or building your own facility. If you are just starting out, I highly recommend renting over buying as a first step. You have the opportunity to see what foot traffic looks like in your area, figure out the ideal set up for YOUR clinic, and get your business up and running without a huge loan.

If you are going with a clinic based model make sure you read the lease agreement carefully. In fact, I would recommend consulting with a lawyer and have them explain it to you. This may seem extreme but commercial lease agreements are different than private housing agreements. You really want to make sure you know what you are signing when it comes to the lease and terms.

There is a growing trend of renting a room in a Cross fit box, yoga studio, or with a group of like-minded health care professionals. This option is a great way to keep your rent down while you are starting up your new company. However, you also need to be careful of any expressed or implied agreements that are made with another business owner.

For instance, if you are opening your clinic with like-minded professionals, what are the agreements about referring to other providers in the same group? Can you count on them to send you people and will they expect the same in return? Are these providers you are comfortable sending clients to? Will payment for services be all cash based, all insurance based, or a mix?

If you are opening a clinic in a gym or studio, will you have an opportunity to provide workshops for the clients there? Will the owner help promote your services? Can you put signage inside or outside the gym so people can find you?

Renting a room can be a great place to start and get your feet wet in this new business venture. Hopefully, you will be growing out of this space and ready to move into your own thing eventually. But this gives you the time to consider your options, look around for just the right place, and consider all of the alternatives.

Perhaps you have thought about opening a clinic out of your house. This is very popular for people who have split level houses or an office area right at the front of their house. Or perhaps a basement that can easily be converted into an office. There is a local Pilates instructor who converted her basement into a beautiful studio. She is located right on a lake with beautiful views from the sliding glass doors. And her commute is amazing!

You would need to check in with your HOA (if you have one) to see if this is even allowed where you live. You need to consider your safety as there are people you may not have met coming to your house. A home based provider would need to find the correct insurance to cover both their home and their business. You need to consider if your house is in a good location for people to easily access. You can be the best Physical Therapist in the entire world but if people can't get to you easily you will have difficulty getting patients.

Mobile based services give people the opportunity to be treated in the comfort of their own home or office. This is a pretty easy set up as your equipment needs are minimal. One light weight but sturdy table is the main equipment requirement. And a reliable car or bike to get from place to place. It is extremely convenient for the clients but certainly requires more leg work on your part. However, I know many successful mobile based practices that continue to choose this form of practice over a one location clinic. This may be just the way for you to get started on your side hustle while you are working to build enough clients for a clinic based practice.

What is concierge Physical Therapy?

Some therapists have heard the term "concierge Physical Therapist" and wondered what that means. Well, the truth is the meaning is held by the person who is saying it. In general the word "concierge" is used to describe a mobile type practice where the therapist comes to you. If you are in a discussion with another PT and they describe their company as concierge, this is most likely what they mean.

However, there are some clinic based companies that also use the term concierge because they offer one-on-one services to their clients. Their practice focuses on delivering that higher level of service or the "concierge" level to each person.

Point being – if someone tells you they have a "concierge" practice they are most likely referring to a mobile practice. But, you could always follow up with "does that mean you go out to the clients home?" which will start a great discussion. Chances are you will learn something pretty interesting.

If you are opening a clinic, where should your space be?

Finding just the right space to open your new Physical Therapy clinic can certainly be a challenge. The first thing to look at is where are the people you are wanting to serve? Or how can those people get to you easily?

I live near Seattle where we have a new high rise going in each day it seems. In the city, PT's have found great success being located in the high rise. They advertise extremely locally to the other people who work in that same high rise. In general, they are open during normal work times and closed on weekends when no one is in the building.

Also in Seattle we have some small and funky little neighborhoods. In general, Seattle-ites prefer to get treatment very locally. They don't like to travel too far. I know several companies that have opened small clinics in these little neighborhoods and also found great success. They are usually smaller store front type operations although now we are seeing an influx of the store on the bottom, condo upstairs type buildings. In the city, look for where the people you want to serve are.

In the suburbs, where I live, people are tired of commuting. Either they think that Seattle is crazy far away (one hour without too much traffic) or they commute to Seattle every day and are tired of driving. My current location is right on the main thoroughfare that leads into and out of town. Most of my patients are from the local community and want to see someone who is located very close by. However, I do have some people who drive from other cities and they appreciate that I am located on a main thoroughfare. So it is easy for people who are local, easy for people who are commuting on a daily basis, and easy for those driving in to town just to see me.

If you are opening a clinic in a small town you may have some of the same issues I deal with. Or there may be a part of town that is heavy with medical-type buildings that you want to be near. You may decide to do a mobile practice because people really don't want to drive in to town. You may decide you want to be in the center of commerce region where people are coming to shop on a regular basis anyway.

Where you live can dramatically influence where you want to open your clinic. It is important to think about who you want to serve and what will be the most attractive location for them. Then start pounding the pavement and see what you can find. This is a great time to connect with other health care professionals and see if they know of any spaces opening up. I actually found my space before it was on the market because of my fellow health care professionals. Or you may want to start meeting with gym and studio owners to see if they have some space available. This is a great opportunity to get out there, meet people you want to be connecting with regarding your business, and find just the right fit for your new business.

What type of space are you looking for?

When you are determining the space you are looking for, it is very important to know who you will be serving. This determines what the space requirements will be for you to open your clinic. Before you go knocking on doors looking for clinic space you want to have your basic requirements decided.

Now, these may not be super specific requirements. Everyone is different in what they need and each clinic is different in what they are offering. My requirements were:

1. A treatment room with a door – I was done working behind a curtain
2. My own bathroom – I was done walking down the hall to go potty
3. A laundry room – my husband didn't want me hauling laundry back and forth
4. Windows! I once worked in a clinic that looked like a bomb shelter with very small windows. I need to look over at my trees across the street throughout the day.

These may not be your requirements but they were what I was going to need in order to work in that physical space all the time. So, when I walked into a space that had already been built out as a Physical Therapy clinic with two treatment rooms, a front office, waiting room, laundry room, a bathroom, and huge windows in the gym, I signed the contract on the spot.

So what do you want in the physical space you will be working in? You may think back to previous locations you have worked in. What did you like about that physical space? What didn't you like about that physical space? This is your chance to find exactly what you want or something that will do for now. You are in control of this decision.

If you are opening an orthopedic clinic, your requirements may be simple. You may just need a table in a room with a box of Theraband. Or you may need to be located in a gym so you can get out of your room and use their gym as a treatment space. This would help increase your exposure and you get the bonus of free equipment to use.

Or if you are opening a pelvic specialist clinic you may be focused on finding a space with more privacy. Perhaps you need to have your own bathroom in the clinic so people don't have to walk down the hall. You may want access to a sink so you can wash your hands before treatment. If you use equipment, you may require more room to fit all the equipment. Or a storage area for the equipment so you can wheel it from room to room.

Whereas a pediatric clinic is certainly going to need some room. You may want one huge open gym space that you can fill with different pieces of equipment. Or perhaps you are looking to have individual rooms for more private sessions with the child and caregiver. In this case you might need a large storage area for all the equipment. If you want to install a swing from the ceiling, you would want to cover this with the landlord prior to signing the lease.

As you can see, what you are looking to focus on treating, who you want to serve, and your own personal preference greatly influence the decisions you make when finding a space. This process can take a while or you can grab the first place you find. I was lucky enough to find a space that exactly met my needs on the first try. However, knowing what you are looking for will greatly help you in making a decision. Here are some questions for you to work through before you go shopping for a space:

1. What are my most basic needs when it comes to treatment? A table, a room, a clinic?
2. What is the easiest way to fulfill those needs?
3. How much room do I need to treat the way I see as best?
4. What equipment do I need access to on a regular basis?
5. Where is the population I want to serve?
6. Is there a room I can rent from someone else? Think doctors, chiropractors, acupuncturists, naturopaths, yoga studios, gyms, cross fit boxes, running stores, spas?

Once you have answered these questions get out there and start looking for your space. This step may take moments or it may take months. Don't let that stop you from moving forward with your plan or this book. Do define what you are looking for and start searching for it. Your perfect location is waiting for you.

4

WHO ARE YOU?

You are doing a great job! You have already decided on a name and created a logo that fits. You know what you are looking to build and have a general idea of the five year plan. You have decided what kind of space you are looking for or opted for a mobile delivery system. Now it's time to get really clear on who you are.

Why is it important to know who you are?

This helps determine who you want to treat. It will help keep your messaging clear when you build your website and start marketing. And it helps you to connect to those you are meant to serve.

Now, I now that you are thinking "I am a Physical Therapist. I can help everyone of every age with an orthopedic, neurological, post-surgical issue." Unfortunately that thinking will get you absolutely zero patients. Why? Because very few people actually know what a Physical Therapist does!

Think about it for a minute – what do you do? Now, send out an E-mail to a few fellow Physical Therapists and ask them what they do. Are the answers the same? Have you read the Vision Statement from the APTA:

"Transforming society by optimizing movement to improve the human experience"

Do you agree that is what you do? Do you think that any potential patient is going to understand what that means? And do they even care what that means? Is this what you are going to put on your website?

I do agree with the APTA that we are movement specialists and we, as Physical Therapists, are primed to help people improve their movement through their space. That improving movement will help improve people's interaction with the world and get them back to a life they love living. But that's not what is on my website. Because the general population does not understand that. Also, I do not want to treat every single person with a movement dysfunction.

To be very specific, I want to help people in the Maple Valley area who have low back and neck pain that is keeping them from what they want to do in life. That's it. Those are my people. Do I also treat shoulder pain, knee pain, TMJ problems, pelvic floor issues? Yes, I do. However, my website and all my advertising is geared toward those with low back and neck pain. Those are the people who are not being served well in my population. I have unique training specifically to help those people. And I enjoy seeing them get back to doing the things that they love to do.

You see, it's like a pie. The pie is all the people in your area that could benefit from Physical Therapy services. I assure you that there are more people who could benefit that don't even know they could. There are more than enough patients to go around.

So, I have decided that my flavor of pie is to offer hands on treatment with specific exercises targeted to their exact problem. My patients do not do hours of a home exercise program. They do about 15 minutes once or twice a day because the exercises are specific to their problem. We are focused on exercises that get them back to the activity they want to get back to.

Now there are some people who do not like being touched. They want to go to more of a gym-based Physical Therapy program that allows them to work out the entire time. Or they are looking for a pediatric clinic with equipment that is focused on children. Or they need neurological rehabilitation that is focused on repetition. These are not the people I am meant to serve. These are not my slices of the pie.

Now it's time to do some really hard work. You need to find your creative space where you can really dive deep into these questions. You may need to read the rest of this chapter and head outside for a walk, run, or hike. You may need to curl up in your favorite chair to start writing. Wherever you need to be is fine but make sure you complete the following BEFORE you set up your clinic. These will remain your guiding principles as you make decisions moving forward.

Now, will these things change over time? Perhaps they will. As part of my annual planning each year I sit down and review my mission statement, vision statement, and core values. This gives me an opportunity to see if they are still as clear as possible and remain in line with the choices I am making on a daily basis. In fact, after I completed year 2 of my company, I printed up my core values and placed them all over my front office. This way I was looking at them daily and could make changes on them as I needed. After a couple of weeks I felt that I had refined them to really reflect what I want PT4EB to be. Give yourself permission to evolve over time but plant your feet firmly now.

Mission Statement

Your mission statement reflects the personality of your

company. It discusses your values and the specific attributes of your company. In general, if you are the only one working for your company then this statement is going to be reflective of who you are, what you value and see as your purpose in building this company. Which is a great place to start. As you grow, you may need to change your mission statement but don't get bogged down here. Create something that is accurate for now and move on.

You can search the internet for "mission statements" and get distracted for hours by reading what other people have written. There are some really great ones for a variety of company sizes. But it is also not reflective of who YOU are and what the mission of YOUR company is. So I don't recommend that for now.

Instead, answer the following questions to create your Mission Statement and move on to the Vision Statement.

Mission statement questions:

1. Who do you serve?
2. How do you serve them?
3. What is unique/different about how you serve them?
4. What do you value?
5. What is your overall goal?

You don't have to answer all those questions in your Mission Statement but it gives you a good starting place. Answer those, write your Mission Statement, and move on. Don't get bogged down with this. Remember that you can always change it over time as your company evolves.

Vision Statement

Remember that 5 year goal we talked about earlier? Where do you see your company in five years? Well this will come in to help you write your Vision Statement. Your

Vision Statement is where you see your company. It may be in five years, ten years, or twenty years but where are you headed? What is the future company you are looking to create?

Again, this is important because you will make decisions based on your Vision Statement in the future. For instance you may have a nutritionist approach you who wants to partner with your company. Is this a good partnership to consider? Well, you can look at your Vision Statement and see if that moves you towards that vision.

Your Vision Statement will also evolve over time so don't get stuck here. Answer these questions, write your Vision Statement and move on. Just remember to re-visit it every so often to decide if it remains accurate or needs to be modified. Once you have evolved it to be exactly what you want it to say then you are able to stand firmly by your Vision Statement when making decisions.

Vision Statement questions:

1. What do you want your company to be known for?
2. What would you like to achieve with your company?
3. What would success look like?

One more step to creating your guiding principles for your company and your decision making process!

Core Values

Now that you have determined your Mission Statement and Vision Statement, you are ready to define the core values that are going to get you there. Core values give you the day to day focus to achieve the mission and vision for your company. These are the ones you will focus on on a daily basis to ensure the train is staying on its tracks. They are also the ones that will need to be communicated clearly to employees so they are carrying out your mission and vision.

These are the action steps, if you will. You can have one core value or twenty. It's your company and you get to decide. However, it can be hard to keep them all in mind on a daily basis if there are too many. You may want to stick with five to eight core values to start with. Remember, don't stay here too long but do make sure you take the time to ensure these core values accurately reflect your company.

Core Values questions:

1. How do you want people to feel when they visit your company?
2. What do you want people to say about your company?
3. How do you decide on your treatment?
4. What makes you special?
5. What is important about your company?
6. What is unique about your company?

For your core values list it may be helpful to use the "sticky method" technique. To utilize this technique find a pad of sticky notes that are the same color. As you answer the questions above, write down each answer on one sticky note. Please write down EVERY answer you can think of to each question above. We will whittle them down in a minute. Just get everything out right now.

Place each sticky note on your desk, a white board, or a cabinet. Somewhere you can see them all laid out. Once you have answered each question and written everything you think you can write, it is time to start organizing. Start moving the sticky notes around so they are in order of priority for your company. You may find that multiple sticky notes say the same thing. Stack these sticky notes on top of each other and take note. If you wrote it down multiple times – it is important to you and your company!

Once you have all your sticky notes in order of importance, evaluate the top ten. Are these going to make the cut to your list of core values? Get rid of any sticky notes that did not make the top ten. Those are not your priorities right now. Out of the top ten are there any that you can let go for now?

You may have found that your core values are all catch phrases or loosely defined terms. That is fine. Once you have gotten the list down to five to eight (ten if you must) core values then you can officially document them in writing or by typing up a document. When you do this feel free to flesh out what that idea means to you.

Remember, there are no right or wrong answers here. You get to determine your company's core values. I intentionally am not putting a list of values in this book because that is irrelevant. My values are not yours. Plus, my core values will probably change next year and I don't want you to hold me to them.

Why are the Mission Statement, Vision Statement, and Core Values so important?

One day I received a phone call from woman looking for treatment for her brother. He has ALS and was driving to Seattle for treatment twice per week. She had been recommended to me by a former patient who was so kind as to brag about the treatment she had received. Now, I very clearly am an outpatient Physical Therapy clinic with an emphasis on manual therapy. After talking with the woman, I clearly saw that she was looking for a gym based supervised exercise program for her brother. By happy chance we have a Physical Therapy clinic in Maple Valley that IS a gym based supervised exercise program clinic. I happily referred her down the street where her brother could receive the services he needed.

Right now, I have minimal equipment in my clinic and was not the best provider for this patient. Because I stand clearly by who I am and what I do, this was easily identified as I asked her what she was looking for. I have also looked around and analyzed my competition to find their strengths in order to refer to them appropriately.

Which is the next step for you as well. Now that you stand very clearly by who you are, what you do, and who you serve, it is time to look around your town and see who else is out there. Do NOT do this before you are clear about what you offer. But make sure you do this before that phone starts ringing.

Remember how I said before that if you can treat everyone you will attract no one? The road to happiness does not involve treating everyone who walks through your door. Nor is that a good business model. I assure you that for every patient you send down the street to a more appropriate clinic you will receive a multitude who benefit from exactly what you have to offer.

So what does the clinic down the street from you do really well? Who can you send their way? How can you create a cooperative working environment for the benefit of everyone in your town?

I worked in Maple Valley for a couple of years before I opened my clinic. I had the opportunity to get to know the other clinics around me. I knew how they treated patients and which patients they treated well. I knew how their clinics were run and who specialized in what. I talked with the managers of local clinics to figure out where their strengths were so we could refer appropriately.

I already mentioned the clinic in my town that has a huge gym for people to work out in. They are staffed during the day by personal trainers who can interact with the clients and be the eyes on the ground. Since there are also Physical Therapists nearby I knew that the person with ALS would be safe there. Whenever I know that people are going to need to access equipment for a long period of time and won't join a local gym, I send them to this clinic. Now, I also know that this clinic recently sold to a larger hospital based organization. So I will keep my ear to the ground to see if all these things remain true or if there are any changes with the new owners.

Right across the street from them is a clinic that has a detailed concussion protocol. Can I treat concussions? Sure, it's not really all that difficult and I have taken some classes in it. But have I taken the time to write up a clear protocol? No. In general, I do not believe in protocols because I find them too restrictive. There is research to indicate that clear protocols are helpful in case of concussion. It makes conversations between athletes, coaches, and providers very clear. Therefore, any potential clients who call regarding a concussion go down the street to that clinic.

The clinic that I used to work at has a variety of therapists with different strengths. There is one who is very hands on in his treatment. Another provider creates extensive home exercise programs for his patients. A third provider focuses on posture and breathing to help patients. These are all things that I also work on in my clinic. However, my former clinic accepts insurance which I do not. If I have a patient who contacts me and is unable to complete a cash-based plan of care, I refer them to the person at my former clinic who is the best match for that patient. By knowing each of their strengths, I am able to make an appropriate referral.

There is one other clinic in my area that is a big chain. The live up to the label big box clinic. They run their clients through protocols based on the diagnosis from the doctor. I receive many patients who have formerly been treated at this company. That's all I have to say about that.

When I was going through my PhD program my instructor Brad Jordan told us: "If you own your own clinic, the best thing that can happen to you is that a better Physical Therapist opens a clinic down the street". We were shocked by this statement until he explained to us that competition keeps us learning, striving, and refining. This makes us better therapists which improves outcomes for all of our patients. This improves the reputation of Physical Therapy in our communities and across the country.

Once you have figured out who you are make sure you figure out who the other local clinics serve. Let's keep our eyes on the fact that there is enough pie for everyone and staying in our lane ends up helping more people. Which is the main goal of all Physical Therapists.

Don't complain about the clinic down the street. It makes you look petty and bitter. Point out their strengths to others. Describe how your offerings are different. Let's work together to improve Physical Therapy as a whole.

Congratulations! You have now completed the hardest parts of setting up your own company. You have figured out who you are and who you serve. You have decided on a name and gotten a logo. You are well on your way to finding just the perfect location to launch this new venture. You have taken care of all the hard stuff and the rest is just logistics.

Remember, don't get bogged down in the decision making. Spend some time in due diligence to make sure you are making the best decision for you and your future company. But don't wallow in indecision for too long. Make a decision and move on. Most likely it won't be the decision that makes or breaks you long term.

5

LAWYER UP / FINANCIALS / PROFESSIONALS YOU NEED IN YOUR LIFE

BUT FIRST, a disclaimer: I am not a lawyer and I am not a bookkeeper. I am merely presenting the things that I wish I had known before I opened my clinic. Proceed with caution!

The legal aspect to setting up a company is the same no matter which flavor you go for. If you are clinic based, home based, or mobile the same legal requirements apply to each situation. There is paperwork that needs to be completed in order for the state and federal governments to know that you are a company. But before you can do that paperwork you need to decide if you are a PLLC or an S-corp.

PLLC versus S-corp

With all the options that are out there, how did I narrow it down to PLLC versus S-Corporation (S-corp)? That part was relatively easy. I was starting out as a sole proprietor – just me, myself, and I. These are the two options that are available for small companies.

Why do I have a PLLC versus LLC here? It is my understanding that Physical Therapists are required to have a PLLC versus an LLC because we have a professional license. Our license requires us to take a national exam and be registered with the state government. We are professionals due to that state license requirement. So, we would have a PLLC versus a LLC.

The PLLC and S-corp are both handled as flow through companies for tax purposes. So, the company earns "x" amount of money each year. You have expenses that are taken out from this amount. One day you pay yourself a salary and that is counted as an expense (oh, happy day!). The rest of the money is profit. This entire profit will flow through as income on your taxes. This is why both the PLLC and S-corp are called flow through companies.

How are the PLLC and S-corp different? The simple answer is the initial paperwork set up is different and they are handled differently for tax purposes. The difference in tax handling doesn't occur until you hit a certain mark. My understanding is the mark is $100,000. When you are earning over $100,000 you should be an S-corp.

But, is that $100,000 how much the company brings in? Or is it how much profit there is? Or is it just a completely random number? The truth is that I don't know and it's difficult to find out.

See, neither a lawyer nor a CPA can tell you how to set up your company. It is outside their professional abilities. Much like us and surgeons. A Physical Therapist cannot tell you need surgery. But we can spot someone who is not responding to treatment the way we think they should. We can recommend that they see their referring physician and talk to them about their lack of progress. We can write a Progress Note to this doctor and explain that their results from therapy are not consistent with the normal results. Then that doctor can refer them to see a surgeon.

This is a decision that you have to make on your own. It's a big decision and it's scary because we are so out of our element. We understand the laws regarding Physical Therapy but taxes and setting up a company? Not our strengths usually. And we can't even hire someone to make the decision for us. Trust me – I tried!

What I have found consistently since opening my clinic is that most people start as a PLLC. Later, you may need to file additional paperwork to change your status to a S-Corp. But that is once you have grown and hopefully money is easier to come by. Again, this is just experience talking and each person needs to make this decision for themselves regarding their company.

How do I file the paperwork?

Now that you have made the decision on what type of company you want it is time to do the legal leg work and make it official. You have three options at this point: hire a lawyer to do it for you, use an on-line resource, or do it yourself.

I will admit that I am extremely biased here and I will push my opinion on you. Hire a lawyer. Trying to do legal paperwork on your own is like our patients consulting Dr. Google because they can treat themselves. And we all know how that works out, right? Don't do that.

Also, it gives you the chance to meet and support a local small business. My lawyer used to work an hour away with a big law firm. She wanted to be closer to her children and serve in her local community. Which is exactly the same reason I opened my clinic! We had some great discussions about our dreams while going through the process of dealing with the paperwork. It's nice to find an ally when you are starting out. Starting your own company is hard. Start building your network.

My lawyer also encouraged me and helped me join the Chamber of Commerce. This is a great group to get to know for local business owners like me. Again this has helped to build my network and meet other people who were just starting out and find mentors who have been rocking it for years.

Plus I truly believe that when we are willing to hire professionals to help us in our business it flows out through our company. After all, we expect people to pay us to help them because we are professionals. WE should practice what we preach and be willing to pay others for their professional knowledge. I'll get off my soap box now.

There are also websites where you can hire people to do all this paperwork for you. LegalZoom is the one I have heard of most often. Most people do not have problems using an on-line lawyer as the paperwork for setting up a company is pretty clear cut. However, you can't see the person face-to-face if you do find any problems. Just a thought.

If you really want to save money, you can do the paperwork yourself. All of the paperwork is available on-line. State and federal governments have websites that offer the forms and instructions for how to fill them out. Although it will take more of your time to fill them out, it will save you money.

Speaking of money

Even before you open your doors, you start spending money on your company. Make sure you keep all of your receipts because you will want to account for this during tax time. I mean *all* of your receipts! For instance, we built my website before we had opened a bank account for the company. I paid for the initial web hosting on my personal credit card. That receipt was then able to be put into Quickbooks as an expense for the company. But I am getting ahead of myself.

Tax time comes April 15th every year whether you are an individual or a small business. The challenge is being prepared for it with a new business. I started my business in

August so I didn't have a complete year full of receipts to deal with. But you want to make sure all your ducks are in a row before tax time.

Again you have the option of hiring someone to do this for you or doing it yourself. The same principles apply as we discussed with hiring a lawyer. You can choose to hire someone to do it correctly or to take the time to educate yourself on how to properly document and itemize. You can even file your taxes on your own.

For the protection of my company and my personal assets, I hired both a bookkeeper and a CPA. The bookkeeper deals with the day to day flow of income and expenses. She categorizes them correctly and asks me if she has any questions. I recently bought two desks from an appliance store and had to send her a note regarding that. Yes, it looks like I bought myself a stove but really I bought two desks. I got a great deal, too.

The CPA deals with the tax side of things. She sends me a list of reports that I need to bring to our annual appointment to file taxes. This includes reports that are sent over from the bookkeeper. I don't understand what these reports are so I just send my bookkeeper a note and say "I need this sent here" and she does it. It's magical! The CPA does the taxes and tells me how I need to adjust my tax payments for the next year. Again, I don't completely understand all this but that's why I hired professionals. They tell me what to do so I don't get in trouble with the government.

I know that some people opt to do their bookkeeping and their taxes on their own in order to save money. I get it! This stuff is expensive. But bookkeepers and CPA's are expensive because they have the knowledge to file things correctly and protect our butts from making mistakes. I have opted to hire professionals from the beginning to take that load off my plate.

If you are doing everything on your own, how can you expect to build a company? Find a network of people who can help you and be grateful to have them surrounding you. Hire them early so they can make sure you start on the correct path.

What if you have the desire to start a company but literally have no cash on hand to do it with? A lawyer, bookkeeper, CPA, rent – these things add up quickly. Some people may have the desire to go out on their own but no nest egg to hatch the plan with.

Can I get a business loan?

So, how are you going to pay for all this? Drain your savings account to live your dream? Or is it time to go see if you can get a small business loan? I used my savings account to open my clinic but I talked with a banker to find out about how to obtain a small business loan for you.

First off, my banker emphasized that the time to talk with your bank about a small business loan is the moment you begin thinking about opening your own business. He emphasized the importance of the relationship with the banker in the decision making process to offer a small business loan. So if you are reading this and realize that you are going to need to take out a loan then you need to be meeting with bankers. Here are the three things he said you would need to apply for a loan.

#1 **Business plan required** – You will have to present a business plan to the bank in order to obtain a loan. This is an extensive document that will help you really define what your company does. In fact, it's a great idea to fill out a business plan even if you don't need a loan. The focus it provides can be amazing!

The Small Business Development Center can help

you to prepare this document. This group helps small businesses in all aspects of business development. They are located at colleges and are an amazing free resource. Find the office near you and go meet with them NOW. It's free and the information they provide is priceless.

On-line you can find resources to help you including bizplantool.com. This is offered through Wells Fargo bank and asks you all the pertinent questions to set up your business plan. It will take quite some time to complete but be a valuable resource to you as you obtain financing.

#2 Two years of financial information for the company – Yes, this one is a sticky point. How do you offer two years of financial information if you are just starting a new company? Well, if you have been a Physical Therapist for at least two years the bank may be able to use your personal finances from your current salary. However, this is not the ideal way for the bank to obtain financial information. This is the biggest hurdle to overcome for small businesses.

The Small Business Association may help to guarantee a loan as a silent co-signer. Basically, they are ensuring the loan with the bank. You will still need to have some skin in the game. The SBA will make sure you have 10-25% of the value of the loan that you are providing.

#3 Paperwork – Once you are ready to apply for the loan the bank is going to want to see all your legal paperwork to make sure that you are able to start the company. All the legal documents discussed earlier will need to be in line before the bank will discuss a loan with you.

The money aspect stops many people from opening their own clinic. It is expensive and you are often putting your finances, as well as your potential earnings, on the line. Many people may stop here and just throw in the towel. But YOU have a vision and dream of what you want to bring to life in your community. There are people out there waiting for you to open your doors and help them get where they want to be. Keep working towards that vision. You may have to take a year to save up the finances to make it happen. You may have to work a sub optimum job to get the money together. This is where it's time to get creative and figure out –how can I open those doors?

6

MONEY, MONEY, MONEY

How much does it cost to open a Physical Therapy clinic?
$12, 656

$12,656 is the amount that I spent to get my doors open. In this chapter we will discuss how that money was spent so you can get a more accurate reading on what your number may be.

You may look at that number and think "That number is much lower than I expected. I can totally do that!" Great! You can move through this chapter and look at the different categories. You can decide where to allocate your resources and be on your way.

But if you look at that number and think "Where am I ever going to find that kind of cash", have no fear. There are many options available. In the last chapter we discussed how you can apply for a loan from a bank. Or you may have a friend or family member who would be willing to loan you some money to finance your dreams. You may have a retirement account that you can draw from. Be very careful with that! Make sure you discuss that with you financial advisor.

You may need to walk through this chapter writing down your amounts. Once you figure out what your number is then you have a goal. Taking an honest look at your finances, see how long it would take to save for that goal. Then you can start chipping away at different aspects of this book while you are saving money.

I know you can do this. There is a drive in you that caused you to open this book in the first place. You have made it this far and kept that motivation going. Don't stop now. Money is not a good reason to stop. There's a way to make your dreams come true. Find it!

The biggest chunk of that $12,656 was spent on rent. In fact, it was almost half. I had to put down first and last month's rent which is pretty typical in commercial real estate. Well, it's just pretty normal nowadays when you are renting!

My clinic did not need an expensive build out. I mentioned previously that there had been a Physical Therapy clinic in my office before it was MY office. So the space was already built out to have a front office, two treatment rooms, a laundry room, and a bathroom. The paint on the walls was horrible. Truly. In one treatment room there were two light gray walls, one dark gray wall, and a brown wall. Seriously, in the same room. My landlord graciously agreed to paint the clinic for me.

I have heard of retail space that requires a significant build out which can be expensive. In my town, a two office clinic space build out can cost $125,000. Right? Anyone ready to dump this Physical Therapy thing and go into construction? But, seriously, build out costs are extremely variable. My build out costs were $0 while my friend who was looking to open an office down the street was going to be $125,000.

Of course if you have a mobile practice you are rent free. This is one of the huge advantages of a mobile practice – the startup costs are much lower than a traditional clinic based practice. Remember, you can always start with a mobile practice and move into a more permanent location over time. There are lots of options.

Rent is also the number one reason Physical Therapists find rooms to rent in doctor's offices, with other health care providers, in CrossFit boxes, or yoga studios. It is much cheaper to rent a room from someone else when you are starting out. And there are no build out costs. It gives you a chance to see if the location works well for you or if you really need to be across town. Renting a room also gives you instant access to those potential clients. Again, this can be a great option that has worked well for many people. You can always move into your own space as you increase your client load or when you are ready to expand.

I chose to rent an entire clinic space. The main reason was the landlord who owns my building. He is a local landlord who really cares about his clients and their businesses. I knew I wanted to rent from him. And the clinic was already built out to my specifications, I didn't have to pay a build out fee. Great landlord + reasonable rent + no build out fees = opportunity I couldn't pass up. Even though starting in a smaller space would have worked initially, missing out on this opportunity would have cost me in the long run.

The second biggest expense was legal documents. Hiring a lawyer to set up my company from a legal standpoint. We discussed this in the last chapter and why I decided to hire someone to do this for me. As health care professionals, I feel we are more open to scrutiny and possible lawsuits. I wanted to make sure that all my legal paperwork was completed perfectly.

Plus, it gave me a chance to meet an awesome small business owner. My lawyer is an amazing person as well as an amazing lawyer. It's great to chat with her regarding her business. She is always very uplifting and positive. Who doesn't need more of that in their lives as a small business owner?

As the receipts started piling up and I didn't know what to do with them all, I hired a bookkeeper to set up a QuickBooks On-line (QBO) account. This was a one time, flat fee agreement where she set up the entire account. She input all my receipts from opening my clinic to give me a proper credit for the expenses my personal savings account had incurred. She also linked all my bank accounts with QBO so it updated automatically. I still had to go in and agree to the credits and debits but it all flowed through independently.

Then I found out about quarterly taxes in the wrong way. I received a letter from the IRS asking why I had not filed my taxes. Of course, I was completely confused because it wasn't the end of the year yet and I had never heard of a thing called quarterly taxes. Which, shockingly, you are required to pay every quarter. I decided at that point that I needed to hire the bookkeeper on a monthly basis so that she would take care of all the things I didn't want to worry about.

Now I pay a flat monthly fee and she manages my books on-line. For the most part, it's a pretty passive process on my part. She takes care of everything and has taught me how to generate my own reports, etc. Of course, she is always available if I should have a question and she sometimes has to ask me how to categorize things. After all, when a $325 charge comes through from an appliance store – it doesn't look like you bought 2 desks. But I did and I have the receipt to prove it!

My bookkeeper also sends reports to my CPA on my behalf during tax time. Honestly, hiring a CPA is a no-brainer in my mind. I consider it basically an insurance policy. I have people who have my back when it comes to making sure that they government is happy with how I am paying them. I don't want to lose my company over a simple mistake that could have been avoided.

Now, CPA's are crazy expensive in my opinion. Because a PLLC and an S-Corp are both flow through businesses for accounting purposes, your CPA will need to do both your professional and your personal taxes. In fact, the CPA's I interviewed all said that they would not do my professional taxes without also doing my personal taxes. Which makes sense since they are so closely linked with both the PLLC and S-corp.

Again, I feel this is an expense that is a must because I want to protect myself and my company by ensuring we are compliant with taxes. You may have some experience in this area and feel comfortable doing your taxes yourself. I do know one local small business owner who has been doing his taxes for 25 years. However, his background is in business and he learned about taxes while he was getting his degree.

Since we are at this point in time, let's talk about those taxes. Next door to me is a great massage therapist who is an amazing person. She has offered me great advice about business over the years. Some of which I have listened to. When I opened my company, Suzie told me that I should plan on paying 1/3 or 33% of my income in taxes. I felt like she was exaggerating. Surely she was overly cautious and trying to scare me.

Well, when the end of the year taxes rolled around I found out that Suzie was absolutely correct. It didn't hit me my first year because I really didn't make money in the 5 months that I was open. When I had one complete year under my belt it certainly did hit me. And hard. I was completely shocked.

At this point, I would recommend you set aside 1/3 of

your income to cover your tax bill as a general rule. If you don't end up paying that amount you can throw a party with the surplus. Or buy some new equipment for your clinic.

Let's take a little detour here and talk about finances and budgeting. This can be really difficult to do from the start of your company. In fact, at two years into running my own company, I feel like I am just starting to get a handle on things. How do you make financial decisions for your company? Do you just plow back any money you make in order to improve the company? When do you start taking salary? What is solid ground you can start making good decisions based on?

I recently read a book "Profit First" by Mike Michalowicz. I wish I had read this book when I started my company because I would have had a solid financial basis to move forward from. I have implemented the "Profit First" strategy in my company and it has had a great effect on how I view everything. I highly recommend you read "Profit First" and implement it into your company.

In the book, Mike explains how you actually need to set aside 15% for taxes. But don't think he has a magic trick for avoiding taxes. He states that you need to start taking a salary immediately. Of course, when you pay yourself a salary you also pay taxes on that amount. You still end up at the 30% mark but it's distributed differently. You should buy that book and keep a copy close by.

The next biggest expense will be your actual equipment. If you are setting up your own clinic, you need to sit down and figure out exactly what you need from an equipment standpoint to open your doors. I had a massage table at my house that was my first treatment table in the clinic. When I had a subleaser in my front office, the massage table became my office desk. It was the perfect sized desk!

Once I had enough money in the bank, I bought a hi-lo

table for the office. This was a necessary expense to protect my body since I am a manual therapist. These tables are not cheap and it may take a while to find exactly what you are looking for.

Start doing your research early if you are looking to purchase or rent equipment. Start searching your local state chapter newsletters to see if there is a clinic in your area that is closing and selling off their equipment. Often you can find equipment on Craigslist from other offices that are closing.

Focus on what you actually need to open your doors. I am still in the process of acquiring the equipment I need to have the clinic I want. I started with a massage table I already had because that was my basic need. My first big purchase was a hi-lo table. Then I needed some storage which came from Ikea. I found a Physical Therapy clinic an hour away that was shutting down and bought some pictures and equipment from them. Right now I have a huge order in for some pulleys and benches. I am looking at purchasing some heavier weights as well. But now I have a profitable company that can afford these bigger ticket items. I believe that my patients will benefit greatly but it wasn't a requirement for opening my doors.

You will also need to furnish a clinic if you choose that route. A waiting room area and a front office with desks, filing cabinets, and a computer. Initially I just found what I could in order to open my doors. Once I had some money coming in I hired an interior designer to do my waiting room. Worth every penny. It looks amazing but I couldn't have done it on my own. I am currently putting together my front office area. I found a corner standing desk that someone was selling on-line. Then I found two other standing desks at the appliance store.

Opting to have a mobile practice or renting a room from someone else significantly cuts down on these costs. You aren't required to spend the time and mental energy up front. You still do need to consider what is required for your company. If you are a mobile practice, you need a strong light weight table. If you are renting a room in a gym or CrossFit box you need to ask if you can have access to that equipment. The answer needs to be "Yes".

No matter what shape your practice takes you will need professional liability insurance. This may take a while to get set up so I would give yourself a minimum of one month lead time to ensure that you insurance policy is up and running on the first day of your company. There are on-line insurance companies and those that probably send you flyers once a month. I opted to get my insurance through a local company. Again, I wanted to support another local small business. To find them, I simply searched on-line for "my town insurance companies" and started calling.

Your future clients need a way to contact you so you need a phone number. I started out using my personal cell phone number but I don't recommend that. Seriously, don't do that. Think about the future. When you decide to grow trying to figure out the phone number thing becomes an obstacle. I should know. I am working on that right now! There are numerous ways that you can get a phone number on-line or a second line added to your cell phone. Or, you can get a physical phone line. There are an infinite number of possibilities here depending on what works best for your plan. I encourage you to think about your five year plan and what you would need at that point. You don't have to start with a plan that robust but look at something that will give you the flexibility to grow.

While you're at it, you should get a fax number. I recommend an on-line option so you don't need a physical fax machine. You can send your notes or bills electronically. Yes, even if you are a cash-based or out of network option you need to have a way to submit documents via fax. Or else you will be required to print them out and go to the post office. Now, I really like my local post office. There are very kind and helpful people there. But I don't want to take time out of day to go down there. Get a fax number. Again, there are multiple options here so a quick on-line search will give you plenty of options to choose from. Faxing options are included in some EMR which may be a feature to look for if you don't want a separate fax program.

Scheduling/EMR

In the next chapter we will dive deep into some of the various options for Electronic Medical Records (EMR). This chapter is focused on reminding you of all the things you need to spend money on. You will need to have some form of scheduling software and a way to document each treatment session. The cost from this varies greatly from $15-$300 per month depending on what you are looking for.

When I originally opened my clinic I wanted my patients to have the ability to schedule on-line to make things easy for them. I did not have a front office person to call and I didn't want scheduling to be a barrier to their treatment plan. However I do not recommend this idea anymore. In fact, the opportunity to schedule independently is slowly disappearing from my website. The reason why? Because patients would decide when they needed to come in and were not continuing with the treatment plan that I had recommended.

How many times have you told a patient that they needed to be seen once per week for six weeks and they start feeling better and want to stretch those appointments out? It may be financial because their co-pays are high or you are out of network. It might be a scheduling issue because they have four kids, three dogs, and two chickens they have to schedule around. Of course, when they show up three weeks later and all their pain has returned they are often frustrated and feel that Physical Therapy is not working for them. In order to have the treatment plan that I have carefully determined is the best strategy to get them where they want to be I am taking away their opportunity to schedule independently.

I understand that you have the best of intentions and want patients to be able to make the best decision regarding their treatment. I understand that we want to believe that OUR patients understand the importance of the plan. I get that we want to help our patients become more independent and take charge of their health. I just don't believe that giving them the opportunity to schedule on their own is the right path to take.

One more thing I wish I had known.

Wow! There are so many different things to spend money on when you are starting and running a clinic. Honestly it feels a little overwhelming at times. And frustrating. Why can't we just keep things slim and trim and pass those savings off to our patients? Well, because we chose to work in health care which requires expensive insurance, proper documentation, and good equipment.

There is an ally that I did not know about when I started my company. A 100% free resource that can help guide you in your decision making while you are starting or growing your company. America's Small Business Development Centers are found at community colleges throughout the nation. They offer 100% free business advice for whatever stage you are at. Coming up with a business plan? They can help! Need to understand marketing? They can teach you. Just need a pep talk? Sure, they do that too. I highly recommend you contact them as soon as possible to get acquainted with your local person. You can find them at: americassbdc.org.

7

WRITE IT DOWN

Yep, even when you have your own place, you still have to write it all down. Even if you are a cash based Physical Therapist, you need to write it down. You may want to set your own rules for your own place but you still have to document appropriately.

Please, do NOT move on from this chapter until you have answered your documentation question. You owe it to yourself to do your due diligence and research. You want to start with the correct system for you from the beginning.

Researching Electronic Medical Records (EMR) systems may not be fun. But having to switch EMR after 6 months because you can't stand the one you are working with is not fun either. Take the time now to look into all the different options. Really think about what you want. Only at that point should you be making a decision regarding which path to follow.

What do you want in an EMR?

Nowadays, EMR are getting fancier. Even doing the research for this chapter I found so many cool features that were not available just a couple of years ago when I opened my clinic. I am sure that there will be even more options in the future.

So my disclaimer – what is stated below was accurate to the best of my knowledge at the time of writing this book. I will be updating this section as we move forward. It is up to you to research the options available and find the right fit for you. I have tried to present an accurate picture of what is available in the market today.

Choosing from the list below is actually pretty easy if you are really clear on what you are looking for in an EMR. To help you with that I have created a couple of questions for you to think about. Remember, when you are answering these questions, you want to look forward into the life of your company in 5 years.

1. Are you planning on billing insurance?
2. Are you planning on billing Medicare (either participating or non-participating)?
3. Do you want an integrated home exercise program?
4. How much are you willing to spend?

Prices vary greatly depending on how robust the system is that you need and how many clinicians you have using the system. The following options are presented from simplest to most robust. In general, they are also presented from cheapest to most expensive. The following list represents options that have been used by people I trust. They are recommended by fellow Physical Therapists. Beyond that I remind you that you need to do your research and find the EMR that is the best fit for your company.

Google Docs

The most basic version of an EMR is creating your own Google document. The nice thing about this is you get to create the version exactly as you want. No more cumbersome EMR with questions you don't want to handle regularly. This is a great option if you are a cash based Physical Therapist. However, if you are planning on billing insurance, especially Medicare, you must have a more robust system.

Acuity Scheduling

Acuity Scheduling is my absolute favorite scheduling software to use. It is easy to use and easy to customize. If you have a question there is a vault of answers. If the vault doesn't have your answer than there are people you can E-mail. I use Acuity Scheduling for my company and I have been extremely happy with them. They are relatively inexpensive and have great customer service. If you are looking to meet the most basic needs of scheduling and documentation, this is the place for you.

IntakeQ

Do you want to build your own intake forms? Would you like patients to fill them out before they come in for a treatment session? Then you will want to check out IntakeQ. You can build your own patient facing forms and send them electronically.

After the visit, you can fill out a custom treatment form to document the visit. Need to send the note to a doctor? There is free E-faxing included with even the most basic package. What I couldn't tell is if you were also able to receive faxes with IntakeQ. That would be an important question if you are going to be receiving referrals from doctors. Most of those are done electronically now.

On their website they also discuss an appointment reminder feature. Which leads me to believe that there is also a scheduling feature but I didn't find it on the website. However, I love that you can create your own intake forms and they are HIPAA compliant. Patients can sign the consent forms electronically. It decreases the need for paper in your clinic.

Jane App

This seems to be the standard entry level EMR for Physical Therapists today. Most of the people I asked liked Jane app and had very positive things to say.

Jane offers a complete scheduling page that looks easy to navigate. You can implement it into your website to offer on-line booking. However I would not offer on-line booking for your patients. I know that it seems more convenient for the patients and for you! No more E-mail chains trying to find the best time. Don't get sucked into that black hole. Trust me. It would be good to have a scheduling link that you can send to patients who are established. It looks like you can do this with Jane.

After the visit you can document the treatment in Jane. One feature that really stood out was the ability to add pictures and/or video right to the patients chart. This could be a valuable asset if you are documenting things such as gait pattern. You could store a video of the patient walking at the first treatment session and then at discharge. That is only one option but would be a powerful testimony for the patient.

Jane does offer a billing to insurance option. This is where things might get a little dicey. I am not sure how robust the billing option is. You would certainly want to check to make sure Jane communicates with the insurance companies you would be billing. However, if you are going to accept insurance from a majority of your patients, I would look for a more robust system that is focused on that aspect.

PTEverywhere

The newest entry into the Physical Therapy EMR is PTEverywhere. In fact, I received an E-mail advertisement for PTEverywhere while I was writing this book. I checked it out with my on-line community and they gave

PTEverywhere rave reviews. Since it is a newer entry into this market, I would expect that their service offerings continue to improve over time.

PTEverywhere is a robust system for a cash based Physical Therapy clinic. To be clear, they do not have an option for billing insurance. That is not the market that they are after. If you are 100% certain that you are going to be billing insurance than please continue reading about one of the other options available.

If you are a cash based clinic than look no further! PTEverywhere offers scheduling software for booking appointments. From that page you can also take payments. They are integrated with a credit card processing company so the payments will show up in PTEverywhere. This may seem like a small thing but it's not. As you begin to grow, keeping track of payments can become more challenging. Having an integrated credit card processing system is really important.

After you finish the appointment, PTEverywhere offers a robust EMR to document what has been done. A really special feature is that you can create a video HEP for the patient. There are tons of videos already available or you can upload your own. Once you create the video HEP, the patient has access to it and can mark it as complete when they have done their exercises. The goal is to increase compliance with HEP performance. I am interested to see if that ends up working. Either way, I like having the video option available that offers a more comprehensive view of the exercises.

PTEverywhere is leading the competition in offering a telehealth option. The future of the medical profession is increasingly going to rely on telehealth – yes, even for Physical Therapists. This is going to allow us to help people who have difficulty traveling to see us. Now, this is not the time to get into all the laws governing telehealth, who can use it, and which patients you can use it for. However, if you are opening a cash based Physical Therapy clinic and looking for a robust system to integrate the scheduling, EMR, payments, and HEP into one place, PTEverywhere is that place. In addition, you get the bonus of adding telehealth in the future.

Web PT

Designed by a Physical Therapist and still run by a Physical Therapist. They are clearly focused on what is needed in the outpatient Physical Therapy clinic that accepts insurance. Web PT is the program that I have utilized in the last 2 insurance based clinics I worked for. Personally I have always been a fan of this company and their EMR.

When I worked with them in the past, the interface into the billing side of the operation was lacking. There was a great amount of difficulty and pain associated with getting things paid. Since then, Web PT has fully integrated with Therabill. I do not have personal experience with the Web PT and Therabill combination but if it works well then this is a strong contender for insurance based companies.

Web PT fully integrates scheduling and EMR. The system is robust enough to allow for the front office to be working in the scheduling while the back office is working in EMR. The EMR was built for and is updated for use by Physical Therapists. I have worked with other systems that are specifically built for other medical professionals. They simply do not work as well for us as a system built for us.

Web PT also offers an on-line home exercise program option. Built by the Physical Therapist for each patient, the patients can download an app to access the program directly on their phone. Again, I am not sure how often patient will actually utilize this feature but I am excited about the option.

Thera Office

Are you still looking for more robust options for EMR?

Thera Office may be the option for you. On their website they state that their system is Medicare compliant. If you are planning on billing Medicare, you need to ensure that your system is Medicare compliant. The Medicare rules are in the process of changing as this book is being written. Start your company off on the correct foot so you don't have to play catch-up moving forward.

TheraOffice offers the complete package from start to finish. Scheduling, EMR, and billing are all contained in this one package. Which you will want if you are billing insurance. Make sure that everything is in one place so you can have everything flow through. Usually when an EMR offers a billing option it is more expensive than an EMR that does not include billing. This is because they constantly have to update the billing side as new regulations are rolled out.

If you are planning to bill insurance, make sure that you have a system that has billing integrated into the system. This will save you time and energy later down the line. However, if you are not planning on billing insurance, you may be paying a hefty price for features you don't need.

A2C Clinic Controller

Just go check out their website: http://a2cmedical.com/. These people mean business. The website is not fancy and there are no bells or whistles. But this system looks to be the most robust option available.

I researched Clinic Controller after some on-line friends recommended it. One has used Clinic Controller for 13 years so far and hasn't found anything better on the market. She even stated that she does check the competition every couple of years.

After looking at their website, I can see why. It's Medicare compliant and a complete EMR system. From scheduling to documentation to billing, it is all in one package together. This system certainly looks to be very solid.

My guess would be that the price tag associated with this system would also be the highest. But, again, if you are going to be billing insurance you want to make sure you have a robust system that is fully integrated. The time and energy you save will make the initial investment worth it.

Make sure you read this part!

Choosing your EMR system takes time and a great deal of research. First you need to do some soul searching and decide what it is you are looking for. Remember all those questions we asked at the beginning regarding who you want to serve and how you want to set up your clinic? That is to make answering the questions of which EMR to choose easier.

Obviously there are very clear options for cash based clinics versus insurance based clinics. Don't buy more than you need! If you are not going to bill insurance you don't need an incredibly integrated system that includes billing. I will add here that WebPT offers Therabill at a separate charge. So you can have the robust system of WebPT without the increased charge of Therabill.

However, do spend some time making this decision. You want to open your doors with the best system for you in place. Changing documentation systems is time consuming and may be expensive. I recommend doing your research now and choosing the best option for you. Time is on your side right now.

There are even more options available on-line. Again, the one described here are the ones utilized and recommended by my on-line community. I tried to present the most popular ones as they have proven to be effective over time. You can go research other options on-line. There are many out there. But don't allow yourself to get stuck in this decision. Set a time that you MUST make this decision or you may be stuck here for months doing research.

Spend the time now to make the best decision but do not let this become a black hole of research that keeps you from moving forward with starting your company. Decide now how long you will spend researching the options. Spend that time doing your due diligence to pick the best option for you. And then move forward confidently with your decision.

8

MARKETING 101

Now that you have put all the pieces in place to open your doors, it's time to let the world know about what YOU have to offer. This is usually the step where most Physical Therapists get frustrated, confused, or just simply overwhelmed. We do not learn marketing tools in school. We are usually not good at sales. Frankly, Physical Therapists are not generally very good advocates for themselves.

Have no fear. We are going to walk through this step by step and discuss the initial phases on marketing. The basics of what you want to have in place when those doors open. I promise you that you can do this. One step at a time!

Remember that mission, vision, and core values stuff we talked about previously? Remember the discussion about your ideal patient and who that was? Who are you building this company to serve? Well, all of that is what you need to keep in mind when you plan your marketing. You need to ask yourself "would this appeal to my ideal customer?" If the answer is YES – then go for it. But, if the answer is NO, then you know to walk away.

For instance, I had been in business for a year when I got

a call from an advertising company that was putting together the programs for the local high school football program. They were offering advertising space in a program that would be handed to every visitor at the football game. Football players are not my ideal patient but their parents are. So I decided it was worth a shot. I got a third of a page ad that was just below the roster. That seemed like good placement!

And I waited for the phone to ring. All season long. I never had one response to my ad. Perhaps the ad copy itself was poor. Perhaps I did not target my ideal customer. Or perhaps no one ever opened the program to see my ad. But chalk all this up to lesson learned and not to be repeated.

One more thing before you get started on working through your initial marketing plan. You will need to decide when you are in over your head and need help from a professional. And you need to be honest with yourself about what point that is. I believe that when we are honest with ourselves about when WE need help, it is then easier for our patients to be honest with themselves about when they need help from us.

Think about it. We are a fiercely independent group of people who are go-getters. We are pretty sure that we can figure all this stuff on our own, eventually, and we work hard to do that. But we are not the BEST at marketing. That is not our skill set and usually not where we are very comfortable.

When we hire someone to help us with the details and shore up our weaknesses, it lifts a huge load off our minds. It allows us to appreciate skills in someone else that we do not possess. It allows us to start building a team around us that we can turn to with questions and needs.

I call this the "Flow of Knowledge". When we allow someone else to teach us something it opens up our communication to teach our patients. We should always be teachers and students at the same time. Just find who can teach you well in what you need to know.

At some points in this marketing section (or in this book!) you may think "Ah, I can do this on my own". And perhaps you can. But is there someone you could hire to do it better? Is there someone who could ease your burden allow you to focus on other tasks? Is it possible to borrow someone else's authority?

Because, all of our patients could just ask Dr. Google the answer to their problem, too. Right? We don't like it when our patients take advice from the internet so let's be careful about doing that ourselves.

#1 – Doctors

If you are opening a traditional insurance based clinic, the usual resource is to take lunch to the doctors. You sit down with them, you tell them how your clinic is amazing, and then you pray that they send you referrals. I would imagine we have all down this song and dance at some point.

However do you want your clinic to be reliant on referrals from doctors? There are so many pitfalls associated with this idea. The doctor may decide to retire or sell their practice. They may get bought out by a bigger hospital group and you will be barred from future entry. They may just decide to start referring to someone down the street.

I caution you strongly to not put all your eggs in this basket. And if you do meet with doctors make sure they are similar in practice to you. If you are accepting insurance, market to insurance based doctors. If you are not accepting insurance, market to out of network doctors like yourself.

Before I opened my doors I met with my number one referral source in my town. She is a great doctor and was incredibly impressed with my unique skill set. I knew if I could get her on board then my company would take off.

Plus, I just really like her as a person and enjoy sharing patients. I couldn't wait to meet with her.

At our lunch time meeting, she introduced me to all the providers in her office as "The Best Physical Therapist in Maple Valley". We sat and talked about my future practice and what my plans/dreams were. She was excited that I was going out on my own until the fateful moment when she asked me what insurance plans I would be accepting.

None. I will be out of network with all insurance.

Well, the meeting ended shortly after that and she kindly showed me to the door. She does occasionally refer people to me even now. But she has told me repeatedly (through patients) that if I was to get a biller and accept insurance then she would have me booked full time.

Learn the lesson here. If you are going to market to doctors, only market to doctors who have the same insurance policy you do. But, truly, don't spend too much time here. You want to get your message out to the world!

#2 – Website

Before you open your doors you MUST have you website up and running. Think about it, how would you feel if your friend referred you to a naturopath and you went to look them up on the internet only to find that they did not have a website. It would be weird. Don't delay. Get your website up and running.

What platform should you use? Do not use a free platform. I know it sounds enticing. You think that it won't really matter and it's so easy. Don't do it. Just trust me on this one.

There are several reasonably priced website builders that you can start off with and they can grow with your company. I have used WordPress and been extremely happy with it. My daughter built my initial website before I opened my doors.

We were able to watch tutorials and figure out how to get the look we wanted.

Remember how I was talking about that "Flow of Knowledge"? Well, after a year I realized that my website looked like it had been put together by a teenager. It was extremely basic and extremely functional. Which worked for me! But didn't help to increase my authority on the internet.

So, a year later I hired someone to create a professional looking website. She did an amazing job. She came in and took pictures of me treating to add to the website. She found some pretty panoramic pictures to put on the front page. She even filmed a video of me for the front page. I definitely stepped up my game.

In addition, a website designer understands SEO. Search Engine Optimization. Don't ask me to explain it because that is why I hired someone to do it. But my website designer got me to the front page of search engines. Which is where you need to be if you want someone to find you.

My website is evolving as I learn what needs to be customized to attract my ideal patient. I wish that I had started with that point of view from the very beginning. It would have saved me a ton of money. Which is why I share this information with you.

Start with a platform that is robust enough to change with your changing needs. Find someone who can help you build a website that speaks to your ideal patient. Write all the copy for your website yourself because you know who you are trying to attract. Make it easy for future patients to find you and learn about you. People may visit your website several times before they trust you enough to pick up the phone to call you. Make sure that website says what you want them to hear.

Should you have a newsletter sign up? Well, there are pros and cons.

The pros – offering a newsletter sign up allows you to start creating a list that you can then use later on to send good content to. You may provide special offers and exclusive benefits to the people on your newsletter list. You are provided access to a list of people who are saying that they want to hear from you regularly. Which gives you a chance to contact them and share your knowledge.

The con (really, I only see one major con with a newsletter list) – you need to send content out to them. Please do not set up a newsletter list and then not contact them. If you are ready to commit, then do it completely. Care for the people on your newsletter list by sending them good information you don't share anywhere else. Nurture them appropriately. They may be your next patient.

You can always wait to set up a newsletter. I didn't start mine until I was a year into my practice and was ready to tackle that newsletter. I had done some continuing education around marketing and was prepared to nurture a newsletter list.

Who do you start with as a provider? The cheapest one I know of is MailChimp. And, by cheap I mean it is free. MailChimp worked for me as a great way to get started and get my feet wet in the newsletter offering. So, if you are just starting to get your feet wet then this is a great place to start.

Once you are more focused on creating multiple lists to do on-line marketing, I highly recommend a paid service. You will have to import your newsletter list over to the new service which can be a slight challenge. But you will have a more robust system that allows you to manage multiple lists. This will become increasingly important once you are ready to do more E-mail marketing.

But, that is all after you open your doors and get your feet on the ground. If you want an on-line newsletter from day one, go with MailChimp. It will be fine for now and allow you time to research and understand what you use E-mail marketing for.

A website is mandatory and you need to make sure it accurately reflects who you are and what you do. People will spend time evaluating you based on what is on-line. What they see will be the difference between if they call you or not. Make sure your message is on your website.

#3 – **Blog**

Offering a blog on your website is a great way to put regular content out there for people to learn about you. It allows them to learn more about what you focus on treating. They learn about your personality from your blog posts.

I highly recommend that you write all your own blog posts. There are now companies out there that will provide content for your blog posts and newsletters. This information is good (great even!) but it doesn't provide your voice to your customers. Write you own blog posts about things that your ideal patient cares about.

Originally, I was focused on providing blog posts about what the research was telling us. I would offer information from the journals and put it in a consumer friendly package. Or so I thought. Until my web designer pointed out that they were not very consumer friendly and were still filled with jargon.

Be careful of the words you use. Make sure your ideal patient will understand them. Have someone who is not familiar with the Physical Therapy profession read them and tell you if they are understandable. Make sure it is not someone you live with. You will be surprised how much of your information has been absorbed by them.

A bonus of blogs is that the search engines like it when you change your website. They see that there is new content and this helps to improve your search rankings. So, write a blog when you are getting started so you can improve those rankings. New websites can take a while to get to the top of the list aand writing a blog regularly can help with that.

#4 – Testimonials are gold!

If Physical Therapists are bad at tooting their own horn, we are worse at asking other people to do it for us. Do it anyway! Having testimonials on your website tell your future customers what past customers have said about you. In their own words! It instantly gives you validity.

This is called social proof. Your patients are providing the proof that you do what you say you do. And, when you are starting out, social proof is the most important thing you can have.

How do you get social proof when you haven't even opened your clinic? Well, have you ever treated a friend on the side for free just because they are your friend? They could offer you a testimonial. Perhaps you have worked with another small business owner in your current position? They would be willing to offer you a testimonial. Use your resources and think creatively. I am sure you have people who have experienced what you have to offer that would be willing to offer you a testimonial.

Ask those precious people to write them down. They can send them directly to you so you can use them on your website or they can leave you a review on Google. Having social proof on the internet certainly increases your authority in the marketplace. Trust me on this – get those reviews as quickly as possible and keep asking for them. I know it's hard but it's going to pay off.

#5 – The paper stuff

By now you have your name, logo, and message squared away. It is time to get some paper to hand people. Why is this a valuable marketing tool? People love to have something concrete to hold onto. It gives future patients or referral sources the feeling that what you offer is legitimate. It grounds people. I am sure there is some psychology behind that, but I know it to be true.

You want to order some business cards. Actually, then you are starting out, you want to order lots of business cards. Start with 1,000. Because the next step is we are going to get you out pounding the pavement and sharing with everyone that your doors are now open. You need to have business cards to hand out to those people.

Don't spend too much time fretting over the cards initially. You will blow through the initial 1,000 and you can make modifications after that. Make sure your logo is on there, the name of your company, your name, and your preferred contact method. Do you want them to call you? Check out your website? E-mail you?

Of course, you could have all of the above on your business card. That's completely your call. Also, think about adding your address to your business card if you are a clinic based company. I did not have that on my first card and it was something that people asked for.

My initial business card I designed myself and ordered on-line. I was very pleased with them as they were simple and elegant. Printed on high quality paper. I enjoyed handing them out.

The second set of business cards I had my designer create for me. I have gotten many more compliments on them. They have all of my forms of contact information on them and yet don't look cluttered. Remember before when we talked about that flow of knowledge? There are people out there who have more experience with these things than we do. What we like may not be what our customers like.

I highly recommend hiring someone to create your business cards. You will end up with a better product that is more geared towards your customer. In fact, I have a notebook where I keep all my ideas for my company. I also keep notes from any classes I have taken. This is my inspiration notebook. And in it I have one page with my old business card and my new business card. It is to remind me that allowing other people to use their knowledge in their area of expertise helps my business grow.

If you are going to be sending professional letters via fax or snail mail then you need to have a letterhead. This can easily be created with your logo, name, and contact information. Again, if you don't know how to do it then hire someone. You have a company, make sure you have a letterhead to send official documentation on.

Many Physical Therapists also want to be able to hand out brochures. Again, it is a concrete piece of material that shows people you are serious. But what should the brochures say? How do you design them? Where should you order them from?

Go back to who you want to treat or who your ideal patient really is. Design the brochure for them. What would speak to them? The words you use will be similar to what is on your website. But, you can't include everything from your website on a brochure. Pick the key things from your website that you want to highlight and work from there.

Once you have your message figured out then hire someone to put it together in a way that is visually pleasing. You may have found a designer locally to work with. Or there are multiple on-line resources such as Fiverr and Thumbtack where you can hire someone for a specific job. Unless you know you have graphic design skills, don't do this alone. You command the content but allow someone else to create the brochure.

#6 – Get out into the community

Now it's time to get out there and spread the word. You are armed with your message of who you treat. You have business cards to hand out to give you something physical to hand out to people. It's time to go find your people!

But where are your people? Well, think about it. You know your people pretty well by now. Where will they be hanging out?

Are they at the Cross Fit gym? Meet the owner of the gym and see if you can offer a free workshop that would benefit the gyms clientele. Do not walk in there empty handed asking for referrals. This rarely, if ever, works. You need to walk in there an offer them value for their people. Why do people drop out of Cross Fit? Do they get injured and not end up coming back? How about offering an injury prevention program specifically for Cross Fit?

Are your people doing yoga multiple times per week? Same thing applies here. What can you offer that is of value to the yoga studio owner. Can you provide a workshop that will appeal to their clientele and help you get in front of people? Are you interested in joining the yoga studio? Trust me, people always have questions when they know there is a Physical Therapist around. I did join my local yoga studio and have reaped the benefits over time. This also allowed me to gain social proof with the studio owner who has allowed me to offer a free workshop.

Are your people parents? You can get your word out there by joining a local health and fitness event at the school. You can offer a fun activity with a sticker as a reward for the children. Meanwhile on the table you are offering a sign up for the parents. If the parents are the preferred patient then make sure it is an event they will also be attending.

What local events do you have in your area that your ideal patient will be at? Can you sponsor that event or have a booth available? In my town I have sponsored a veterans run and had a booth at a cancer walk. There is an extremely popular farmer's market during the summer with a chance to offer a booth there.

I live in a big town that still feels like a small town. My ideal clients like keeping things local. They want to see you supporting events within the community. So my marketing efforts are focused very locally. I do have people who travel an hour to see me and I am grateful for them. But I know that most people will not travel that far for Physical Therapy where I am located. The focus for my advertising is extremely local.

How about meeting with other small businesses? This can be a great opportunity to network but also to learn from other small business owners. Plus, when you are out there on your own, it can be nice to have someone to commiserate with. Where are the local small business owners hanging out? You should certainly visit them and see if they are a good fit for your business.

The Chamber of Commerce is designed to help support small businesses. They can be a great resource in networking and growing your business. You may find other professionals who can help you through their services.

There are service organizations such as Rotary and Kiwanis. See if they are active in your town or nearby and go visit with them. These are small business owners who are focused on giving back to their communities. If that is something that resonates with you then you may have found your tribe!

There are also local networking groups that you can pay to join. The success with these varies. I know some people who have had great success and others who have not received much benefit. It is nice to be with other small business owners who are in the grind with you. I didn't like the high pressure sales tactics they used to encourage me to join them. But the flavor of the group can vary greatly from town to town. Please do visit your local variety and see what you think. If the people are a good fit for your business then go for it!

Is there a health care small business group in your area? I was lucky to have a health care small business group already created in my area. I had met them when I was still working an hour away and kept attending their meetings when I worked for someone else in my town. So when I started my own business I already had some solid credibility within this group. They actually helped me find my clinic space and were several of my first customers. If you do not have a small business group in your town, I would recommend starting one. It's a great way to meet other health care providers, network, get business advice, and have a group of like-minded individuals to connect with.

#7 – What about on-line marketing?

If you have been searching the internet for mentoring on how to start a Physical Therapy clinic then I am sure you have seen information regarding on-line marketing and how important it is for your business. I agree that on-line marketing is how you will grow your business. However, when you are just getting your doors open, it is a distraction. And it is expensive.

Get your doors open and your feet underneath you. Complete all the other steps in this book first. Do your marketing through your face to face interactions and your website. Then, once you are firmly settled in that place, start searching for tools regarding on-line marketing. There are many people out there with some amazing programs.

One step at a time. Don't get distracted by all the shiny objects that are buzzing around in the on-line world. Get all your paperwork done. Focus on understanding your ideal clients. Pound the pavement and get to know your local community. You can do this. Stay focused.

9

NOW TO YOU!

CONGRATULATIONS! You have made it to the final chapter of the book and are now equipped for the beginning of your new journey as a business owner.

You have decided on the name of your company and designed your logo. This is the beginning of the brand that you will create. If you are not 100% comfortable with what you have chosen then spend some more time here. You want to move forward with complete confidence in the name and logo. This is the beginning of building your brand and not something you want to change later on.

You have figured out what you are trying to build which will help to influence how you spend your money moving forward. It determines if you want to be a mobile practice or clinic based practice. Knowing where you are headed determines if you decide to be an in network provider or out of network. Perhaps a hybrid is what works best for you. It's your company and you get to make all these decisions! Lucky you.

Along the way you have figured out who your ideal client is. You have learned how valuable that information is and how you will utilize it throughout your company. It will inform all the decisions you make from here on out. This information will guide you in designing your website. It will also help you to focus in your marketing efforts. Knowing your ideal patient gives you the words you need to appeal directly to them.

Of course, your ideal client may change over time. Which is fine! Just remember that you will then need to change the wording of your website, brochures, and all your advertising. Don't try to appeal to everyone. Be the go-to Physical Therapist for the client you best serve.

By now you have completed (or at least started on!) your legal paperwork. You have decided if you are going to start as a PLLC or an S-corp. You are researching liability insurances to make sure your assets are properly covered.

You are finding other professionals who can come alongside you to help you realize your dream. You may have hired a lawyer, a bookkeeper, a CPA, a web designer, or a graphic designer. You may have hired all of them! One key note about timing here: CPAs usually do not accept new client meetings from January through April as this is their busy time filing tax returns. Make sure you go through that process well before you need them to file your taxes.

Your company may already have electronic medical records (EMR) in place or you may be waiting until you open your doors. But, you have done your research to decide which EMR will work best for your company. The one that offers the features that are the best fit for what you want to offer.

Marketing 101 is well on its way to being implemented. You are actively looking into ways to serve in your local community and get the word out there about your company. Perhaps you are already attending networking meetings, Chamber of Commerce events, or Rotary/Kiwanis meetings.

Find your tribe that will help support you. Learn everything you can from them.

Before you put this book down and get to work you need to be super clear on who you do and don't serve. You should know what services are offered elsewhere in your community so you can make confident referrals. People will trust you more when you are willing to refer out as appropriate. It validates your authority as a quality health care provider.

You have answered tons of difficult questions along the way. Congratulations on answering all those questions. Hopefully they have provided true clarity on what you want and how to get there. If you aren't done with all the questions yet please do go back and answer them. Each of them was crafted to help you become crystal clear on what you are focused on creating with your company.

At this point, you may feel like you want to vomit. That is completely normal! Nothing worth doing ever feels comfortable. It is only when we push the bounds of what we think is possible that we can achieve something new and unique. You and your company are needed to serve those clients that will be best served by what you have to offer.

In my clinic I have a sign that says – "Do not go where the path may lead. Go instead where there is no path, and leave a trail (Emerson)". That is what I have tried to do here. I created my own path with my company. In this book I have tried to create the trail for you to follow to get you started on your own unique journey.

I look forward to hearing about your adventure!

ABOUT THE AUTHOR

Dr. Amy Konvalin is the CEO and President of *Physical Therapy for EveryBODY*, a clinic in the town of Maple Valley, WA. In her second year of business ownership, she replaced her salary from her previous insurance-based clinic jobs. *The PT Business Map*, Amy leads you on a journey to creating a business you love running.

www.ingramcontent.com/pod-product-compliance
Lightning Source LLC
Chambersburg PA
CBHW070437220526
45466CB00004B/1715